The
Naptime
Book

CYNTHIA MacGREGOR

CONARI PRESS

First published in 2003 by
Red Wheel/Weiser, LLC
York Beach, ME
With offices at:
368 Congress Street
Boston, MA 02210
www.redwheelweiser.com

Cataloging-in-Publication Data
available upon request from the Library of Congress

Typeset in New Baskerville by Maxine Ressler
Cover and interior illustrations by Gary Phillips

Printed in Canada
TCP

10   09   08   07   06   05   04   03
      8   7   6   5   4   3   2   1

For Laurel . . . always

Contents

Acknowledgments

Thanks to (alphabetically): Cynthia S. Potts, Leslie Rossman, John Wasukanis, Tiff Wimberly

Introduction:
Even Without the Closet Monster

Bedtimes and naptimes. They share so much and yet in ways they are dissimilar, too. In both cases, you are trying to get a child to go to sleep—primarily because the child needs to rest and secondarily because (let's be honest), *you* need a break too! When your child is down for a nap, *you* can catch a nap yourself—or at least catch your breath, maybe get tonight's dinner started, or "pick up" the living room so it no longer looks like it was visited by a deranged tornado. (See the chapter, "Time Out for Mom, Too!" for a little more on the subject of making good use for yourself of your child's naptime.)

Kids resist going to bed at night for many reasons. Fear of the dark—and of the imagined bugaboos that await in that darkness—is a prime one. On the other hand, very few kids fear naptime because of "the closet monster" or "what's under the bed"; in daylight, these kinds of terrors recede. Another reason that lurks behind resistance to going to bed at night is fear of having a nightmare, but very few kids have nightmares during naps.

Yet, even without being concerned over closet monsters and nightmares, many kids resist going to bed for a nap just the same.

Why is that?

One big reason—and it's an operative in avoiding nighttime bedtime too—is the fear of missing something. What are *you* going to be doing while your child is asleep? What's going to be happening in the house and in the world out there that he's not going to be aware of while he sleeps? You may say, "I'm just going to be resting, myself," or "I'll only be in the kitchen, starting dinner," but that's scant reassurance to an active four-year-old for whom every audible fire siren and every squirrel on the tree branch outside the window is an adventure. Even the prospect that *Barney* or *Blue's Clues* might come on the TV while he sleeps—and misses it—is devastating.

You can't in clear conscience promise him unconditionally that nothing exciting will transpire while he's napping. You don't know what neighborhood excitement will erupt, what friend will ring the doorbell, or what else might occur during that time.

The best you can do is make lying down for a nap seem appealing and pave the way for him to relax and rest. And that's basically what this book is about.

Studies state that sleep is important for all of us but especially for kids. The average preschooler needs nine hours of sleep a night, as well as a nap during the day. And I surely don't have to explain that a nap is as important to his disposition as it is to his health! What parent hasn't had to deal with a cranky child who's out of sorts or out of control due to missing a nap or having a nap curtailed?

The aim of this book is to offer you ways to make naptime easier. It's a two-pronged plan: You need to induce your child into getting on her bed in preparation for a nap; and you need to get her to relax once she's there, so she can fall asleep.

In this introduction I'll discuss ways to ease the naptime struggle. Then I'll suggest some activities that you can engage in with your child in or on the bed. These activities have a dual purpose:

1. The prospect of participating in them can help lure your child to his bed.

2. The activities themselves are soothing and/or engaging. They will help relax the child and/or take his attention away from anything that might be troubling him, from a concern about missing something while he sleeps to an even more pressing worry such as an

imminent trip to the dentist, or the approach of his first day in kindergarten or pre-school or daycare.

Besides being concerned that they'll miss something, other reasons kids resist naps are because they want to be "a big kid" and because they simply don't realize they're tired. Kids aren't as attuned to their body signals as adults are. If you're at the end of your rope, if simple tasks are defeating you, everyone is annoying you, and you're just about out of patience, chances are it's because you're overtired and chances are you know it. But the three- or four-year-old who's cranky or racing around the house out of control is probably also overtired but almost certainly doesn't recognize it.

Fortunately you do. If your son or daughter is showing every sign of being overtired, *you*, at least, know what the matter is—and what the solution is. After he has his nap, things will get better.

You can help your cause along by taking the following steps:

1. Try to put him in for his nap at the same time every day. It helps to establish a routine. If your child knows naptime isn't "negotiable," he'll be less likely to try to fight it. If 1:00 or 2:00 or just after lunch is naptime

every day, your child will know that it's naptime and he's expected to go inside and lie down and close his eyes. Making one of the activities in this book part of a pre-nap routine should help. If the child knows the routine involves something enjoyable and is not just a boring, loss-of-playtime nap, he's more likely to be acquiescent.

Do not, however, be such a slave to routine that you go to either of the two extremes. If it's fifteen minutes before your child's usual naptime but he's clearly tired, it won't throw his whole routine off if you put him in for his nap fifteen minutes early today. On the other hand, if you have company whom your child is involved with and you know they're going to leave soon, it's better to put your child in for his nap fifteen minutes or half an hour late than to try to break up his visit with his cousin and force him to go lie down. Routine is a good thing; but so is a reasonable amount of flexibility.

2. Limit her intake of sugars and other stimulants in the hour or so before naptime. Though science is still not in complete accord about the role sugar plays in turning kids into whirlwinds, more scientists and doctors seem to believe the theory than not; what's the harm in playing safe? I don't suppose a dish of chocolate pudding is

going to totally ruin her chances of falling asleep or even settling down and trying, but does she really need that candy bar or glass of soda before her nap? It can wait until afterward.

3. Speaking of waiting till afterward, in extreme cases you can always try promising him something good—a sweet or a story, a game, or something else he enjoys—if he naps or at least stays in bed for a set amount of time. Okay, this is bribery, but you know what? Bribery's been around for so long because *bribery works.* And if your child is so nap-resistant that the only way to get him to lie down is to promise him a treat for afterward, you can promise him something minimal—or something you were going to give him anyhow. As long as you don't use bribery to get him to do every single thing you want, from cleaning his room to taking his vitamins to being nice to his siblings, there's no harm in occasional bribes.

4. Right after lunch is often a good time to put a child in for a nap. The body is more sluggish anyhow since it's busy digesting food and she's less likely to be filled with enough energy to run around the block forty times. As a result, she'll probably be more likely to lie down

without resisting. Also, if she's just been busy with lunch you're not interrupting her in the middle of a fun game, an interesting TV show, or some other activity she's resistant to being taken away from.

5. Draw the blinds when you put him in. Many kids are perfectly capable of sleeping in broad daylight, but others aren't. Too, if his room is on the first floor or otherwise has a view visible from his bed—even if it's only of a tree full of robins and squirrels—you'll eliminate distractions and give him one less reason to fight to keep his eyes open. Also a darkened room is reminiscent of nighttime and suggests his closing his eyes and drifting off. It's subtle but it's valuable.

6. Make naptime comforting. When she was an infant you probably put her in for naps with a bottle and perhaps a stuffed animal. As she grew a little older, she probably still took a stuffed animal with her, and per-haps a "blankie." Now that she's three or four, she may no longer have a "blankie" (though if she does, by all means let her take it in for naps) but she can still take a stuffed animal to bed for naps. And it wouldn't hurt to cover her with a blanket for that secure, protected feeling it gives, even if the room temperature doesn't

require it. In fact, a special "nap blanket" or "nap quilt" can reinforce the idea that now it's naptime.

Some parents go so far as to put the child in her p.j.s and under the covers for a nap. While this does reinforce the idea that sleep is expected, most parents think it's not necessary. Simply lying on the bed—in clothes—is good enough, though lying under a blanket or other covering can be helpful.

Be aware that there will come a time when he outgrows naps. At first he may just fail to fall asleep from time to time when you put him in for his nap. Or he may be more actively resistant: "I'm not tired." "I don't want to lie down." If he's four or five, pay attention. This may not be that old-time resistance; this may be a sincere statement that he's outgrowing the need for naps.

But, for a while, you can mandate a "quiet time," simply a rest period even if he doesn't literally fall asleep. If he lies down, rests, and relaxes, that still accomplishes some good in giving his body a chance to catch up. And it accomplishes some good in giving you a break too.

Tell him you don't necessarily expect him to sleep, but you do want him to rest. The thinking activities described in the chapter "Travels to the Lands of Imagination and

Conceptualization," while offered here as a means to get the child settled into bed and into a relaxed state prior to napping, will also serve well in giving him something pleasant to keep his mind occupied while he rests.

While we're on the subject of napping vs. resting and eventually giving up the practice altogether, let's talk about the child who says she's too old for a nap or who simply can't sleep in the daytime anymore. If she *says* she's too old to nap, she may be telling the truth—or she may simply be trying to grow up quickly. Despite the sentiments of Peter Pan and his band of lost boys who proclaimed they didn't ever want to grow up, most kids are very eager to be "big kids" and then eventually grownups. And if Kim up the street or friend Michael's older brother Jerry no longer nap because they're "too old for that," not napping may seem like a delightfully grown-up concept.

But there comes a time when a child truly does outgrow the need to nap. It usually isn't something that happens overnight. The child may start waking up sooner after lying down for a nap or having more trouble falling asleep at naptime, as well as perhaps being more resistant to the idea of going in for a nap at all. But, at least at first, there will still be days when he needs a nap—and gets oh-so-cranky or out of control if he doesn't have one. Try to get him to at least lie down for a simple rest period, at least for a few more months.

Those naptimes of hers—even if they're now just rest times—are helpful to her, and are equally helpful to you. But take heart—when she does give up naps and resting altogether, you'll probably be able to get her in for bed a little earlier at night. You can even use that as an actual bargain: "You're old enough that I'll let you skip your nap. But you're going to have to go to bed half an hour/fifteen minutes earlier."

But for as long as your child is young enough, he's going to need naps. The purpose of this book is to make naptime easier—a part of the day that the child will at least accept even if not actively look forward to and a part of the day that you won't have to dread. Getting him in for a nap may offer you a break, but it hardly seems worth it if it's preceded by twenty minutes of resistance, of begging and arguing and "I'm not tired!" and "Please let me play for ten minutes more!" and possibly even angry screaming and stamping.

Besides all the suggestions I've already made, what may be the best suggestion of all—and it's the crux of this book—is to tempt her to bed for her nap with an activity that's relaxing and soothing and may help make it easier for her to sleep. And because these activities are fun, they can help persuade her to get onto the bed, where the activity is to take place.

Parents have long been putting kids to bed at night with a story or other bedtime activity. (For more ideas on bedtime activities, see my book *Night-Night*.) Why should naptime be any different? We sweeten the going-to-bed routine for kids at night by settling them in with a story or other activity, why not at naptime?

What follows are some suggestions for pre-nap activities. They'll tempt your child to go to bed when you tell him what you have planned for the two of you as soon as he's settled onto his bed. They'll relax him, too, and distract him from whatever thoughts might otherwise keep him awake. Obviously some are more suitable for younger nappers, others for kids who have developed certain skills and abilities. But, whatever your child's age is now, you're sure to find poems, games, storytime activities, and fun things to think about and imagine that will capture his interest.

May they be of great help to you.

Relaxing Story Activities

The traditional pre-sleep ritual at night is a bedtime story. Certainly, if you're going to do something soothing for your child before a nap, you can't go amiss with a story then either. But as I pointed out in my book Night–Night, *there are many other things that a parent can do for and with a child in lieu of telling her a story; and even if storytelling is your choice of activity, you needn't confine yourself to the traditional reading of a favorite fairytale or other story or book. There are plenty of other types of storytelling activities you can engage in with your child. This section of* The Naptime Book *offers some suggestions.*

Magic Truck Ride

Take your child on a magic truck ride all over the world—without his leaving his bed. The only fuel you need to drive this truck is your imaginations. Though it isn't necessary, you can wear some kind of hat—even just a simple bill cap—and tell him it's your truck driver's hat. Then get him onto his bed, settled in for his nap, and tell him to close his eyes so he can see the pictures in his mind more clearly.

Now describe the truck pulling away from the curb (suitable *vroom, vroom, roarrrrr* noises would help here), and then describe the magic truck leaving the ground and flying up into the air! Describe, at first, your house, which the truck is now hovering over, and then your street, including familiar details.

Then, as the magic truck reaches the end of the street, let the views become more fantastic. Instead of your flying over the familiar next block of houses and ordinary trees, describe trees with purple leaves or orange leaves with yellow polka dots or perhaps with candy canes or lollipops growing on them. Or perhaps, if it's winter in reality, the trees in the next block are in full bloom and warmed by a hot, summery sun.

That next block might be filled with houses made of spun sugar or with palaces, or perhaps there's a mountain or the ocean.

You can end the truck ride after describing just a few more scenes, or you can go further with it, but at some point if your child is not yet asleep tell him, "Now you're going to drive the truck yourself until you fall asleep. Just lie there and think of all the sights you want to see from the truck's windows. Sleep well."

The magic truck can take you and your child on many rides, seeing different sights each time—or returning over and over to some of the ones your child has loved the most in past expeditions.

The Wacky Helicopter

The wacky helicopter is a "cousin" to the magic truck (see page 13), but while the magic truck will take your child to places where she sees fantastic sights, the wacky helicopter will take her places where she has wonderful adventures.

Each time the helicopter takes off (suitable noises, please: *whappa whappa whappa whappa*), your child is off on another adventure. Will she meet friendly beings from outer space? Will she meet Bigfoot and learn the "monster" is really a shy and scared soul? Will she be transported back to the time of Robin Hood and help Robin outwit the Sheriff of Nottingham? Will she be part of Buffalo Bill's Wild West Show and win fame for her rope tricks? Or join the circus? Or be the creator of some wonderful new invention for which the world will thank her and award her a medal? Or meet up with one of her favorite book or story characters and have a quiet conversation with Hansel or Chicken Little or Pinocchio?

All it takes is a ride in the Wacky Helicopter—and a good imagination. Well, two good imaginations: yours and hers.

Alternate Endings

This activity is very simple: Read a story to your child or tell her an old favorite you know by heart. Then ask her "Suppose . . ." and set up a change in the storyline: Suppose the slipper had fit some other girl before the prince got to Cinderella. Suppose the witch's oven didn't work (or was too small for Hansel and Gretel to fit into). Suppose the wolf had found a way to knock down the third little pig's house after being unable to huff and puff it down. What does your child think would have happened then?

Cue, Please

Read (or tell) a familiar story to your child, one he's heard plenty of times before. Stop at several crucial parts in the story. Each time you stop, ask "What happened next? Do you remember?"

When he remembers, praise him. If he tells the story differently than it really goes, don't tell him he's wrong; just say, "Oh, I like the way you tell it. And what happened next?"

You can get the story back on track gently or you can give up on telling him the usual version and simply let him run away with it.

Object Story

In this story game, which requires creativity on your part, your child chooses an object—any object. It can be something you have in your home, something she's seen somewhere else, or something she's heard about. Then *you* have to make up a story about that object.

It doesn't have to be a long or complicated story but use your imagination and make the story more than a few sentences long.

Variation: For a change of pace, *you* pick the object and let your child make up the story.

His Very Own Hero

This activity can carry over from one naptime to another and another, but it requires a bit of prep the first time you do it. Even before naptime, ask your child to dream up a character and say you will tell him a story about the character. Ask him to tell you about the character in advance. If you want to get the child more involved, ask him to draw a picture of the character. You need to know the character's name and as much about him or her as possible. Is he or she a kid, a bunny, a police officer or firefighter, a dinosaur or dragon, a princess or prince, a soldier?

Now, when you tell him it's naptime and he should get into bed, add, "And, don't forget, I'm going to tell you a story about [name of character the child has invented]."

Get the child settled on his bed, perhaps under a blanket or special nap quilt, and begin to spin your yarn. It can be long or brief. It doesn't have to be Newbery-prizeworthy material. It just has to "star" the character he dreamed up.

And from now on, whenever you want to give him a little extra reward or bribe him into napping more willingly, you can tell him a story about his favorite character.

Relaxing Story
Activities

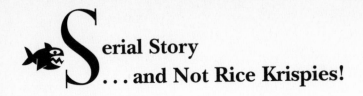

Serial Story
. . . and Not Rice Krispies!

This is a serial story, not a cereal story, so you won't be bringing milk and sugar to bed with your child at naptime—but you will be bringing your imagination. You'll probably also want to do some advance planning though it is possible to "wing it."

For this activity, you want to write a story in advance. Not word for word, written down, but at least general thoughts of who the characters are and what's going to happen to them. You want the story to have at least four "cliffhangers."

On Day One of the story—let's say Monday—you put your child in for her nap and tell her the story. Stop the story in the middle, at a cliffhanger point. It doesn't have to be a throat-gripping, heart-stopping cliffhanger; in fact, it's better if it isn't. It can be as mild a cliffhanger as, "When Jeffrey got up onto the carousel, he could hardly believe who he saw sitting on the big, gold horse!"

Who did Jeffrey see? Your child won't find out till tomorrow, though you can remind her a couple of times on Tuesday morning that you're going to continue the story when she goes in for her nap. And true to your word, you will. Although she'll find out on Tuesday who Jeffrey saw when he got onto the carousel, you're going to end Tuesday's story at another cliffhanger point. Perhaps it will be when Jeffrey, having discovered his grandma from Maine on the carousel, suddenly sees one of the horses wink at him. He asks his grandma if she saw it too, but she hadn't seen it. Just then, the horse's tail twitches. Is the carousel magical? Or is there some other explanation?

Your child will have to wait till naptime tomorrow to learn what happened next and why the horse on the carousel seems to be alive. And of course, even though you reveal that mystery then, you're going to end the day's installment with *another* cliffhanger. So if she wants to find out the answer to what happened then, she'd better hurry up and get ready when you announce the next day that it's naptime!

You don't want to drag these stories out indefinitely. After four or five days or a whole week at most, tell your child, "I'm going to finish the story today. Hurry up and get ready for your nap!" You might want to start another story soon after you end the first one.

Fill in the Blanks

Tell your child that you are going to tell him a story about himself and he is going to help you by filling in the blanks. The first time or two you'll have to prompt him quite a bit. But after that, he'll get the hang of it and fill in the blanks as soon as your voice "hangs" and you pause and look at him expectantly.

You might start with, "Once upon a time there was a boy named ____." Look at your child expectantly with one eyebrow raised, and if he doesn't get what's expected, coach him, "It's your turn. It's a story about you. Fill in what's missing: What's your name?"

Then you can go on, perhaps saying, "He had two older brothers. Their names were ____." And again, if he doesn't pick up on what he's supposed to do, prompt him: "What are your brothers' names?"

The story might continue, "His favorite toys were ____. His favorite food was ____. His favorite stuffed animal was named ____. The thing he most loved to do was ____." And continue on like that.

This "story" doesn't have to have a plot, adventure, conflict, and resolution, or any of the things that make for a good yarn in published fiction. It's enough that you're telling a story about him and that you're giving him a chance to chime in with the "right answers." He'll love it!

"Tell Me a Me Story"

Though not every parent has enough fiction-writing ability to make up stories that are totally original, there are plenty of parents who do just that. Instead of making up stories about elephants or puppies or firefighters or just any old kid, however, why not make up a story about your child? He'd love to "star" in a story!

The more conventional way to do this is: If your child's name is Bryan tell him a story about a boy named Bryan and describe your story's Bryan in such a way that it's obvious you're talking about your child. This is a fine way but I have a different approach.

Start your story this way: "One day you were walking down the street when suddenly you saw a box. . . ."

If you remember your grammar lessons, the conventional way of doing it is "third person"—"he," "she," or "they." The way I'm suggesting is "second person"—"you." Tell your story in the second person and draw your child right into it.

This isn't recommended for the youngest of nappers who might be confused by the second-person format and think the stories are actual events they just don't remember. But try it on your older nappers.

Illustrated Stories – 1

In most storytelling, the words precede the pictures, but in this activity, the pictures come first. Cut a picture out of a magazine. The picture should show either a person or an animal as well as something more. Either the person or animal should be *doing something* (even something as simple as a person looking at his watch would be all right) or should be shown in some surroundings, preferably something more than just a typical living room.

Now show the picture to your child and ask her to make up a story about the picture. You can prompt her: What is the person's name? Or, if the animal is a domestic animal or horse, what is the animal's name? What is the person or animal doing? What does your child suppose the person might be about to do? What does she suppose the person might have just done? If the person is outdoors or in a car or on a bike (or any other form of transportation), where might she be going?

When she answers, you can then ask follow-up questions, prompting her to supply further details.

(When she gets up from his nap, you can suggest she draw more pictures of the people in the story, if she wants.)

Illustrated Stories – 2

For this version of Illustrated Stories, you need to have cut out a variety of pictures from magazines (or advertisements). It's better if you first paste them on cardboard, parts of old file folders, or some other relatively sturdy backing though it's not absolutely essential. Each of these pictures should be easily recognizable to your child. (Examples include a ball, a house, a helicopter, a woman, a child, a police officer, a dog, a lake, a truck, a fire, a group of kids playing, and an apple.)

Now put the pictures upside-down and have your child choose five without knowing what they are. (If he can't yet count to five, you can do the counting for him.) Show him the five pictures and make sure he knows what they all are. Now ask him to make up a story that includes each of the five items in it.

If he's very young, don't be disappointed if he offers you a one-sentence story. ("A boy was playing with a ball when a dog came along with a woman and ran into a house.") As he gets older and as you play this game more often, he'll start offering you more complex stories.

You can ask him questions, too: "What did the dog look like? Did the boy pet the dog? Was the dog friendly? What was the boy's name? Did the dog live in the house he ran into? Was it the boy's house?" In this way you can encourage him to supply more details in his stories.

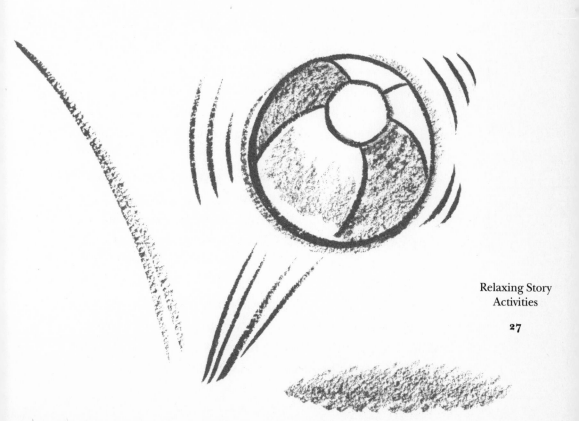

Relaxing Story
Activities

Photo Album Stories

Bring one of your family photo albums into your child's bedroom and flip through the pages slowly, asking your child to pick a picture that she'd like to know more about. This can be a photo album of your child or children, one that contains pictures of you or your spouse as a child, or one that contains photos of members of your extended family.

When your child sees one that intrigues her, tell her as much as you can about the photo or at least as much as you think will interest her. If the photo is of her as a baby, you can tell her approximately how old she was at the time, where the picture was taken, what was going on at the time ("Cousin Ed was visiting with his family—that's his daughter Marie, your second cousin, in the background"), and other details. If the picture is of some other family member, perhaps one she doesn't recognize, tell her who the photo is of. Even if you yourself don't know the circumstances surrounding the picture, you can tell her, "That's Nana Iris when she was a teenager. She grew up in Buffalo, a city in New York State, so that might be where the picture was taken. I don't know who that is with her but it's probably one of her friends."

You can prompt your child to participate with questions: "What do you suppose Nana Iris and her friends liked to do together?"

If she answers, "Play on the computer," or "Watch videos," you can explain that when Nana Iris was a teenager there were no home computers or videos.

If the picture of Nana Iris as a child includes her sister Angie, you can point out to your child that "The other girl with her is Aunt Angie. Did you realize Aunt Angie is Nana Iris's sister? They're sisters just like you and Melody are."

Three Generations

"My, how times have changed!" How often have you heard (or even said) that phrase? Though as a child you may have been tired of hearing stories of the "When I was your age I had to walk five miles to school" variety, I'll bet you were still held enrapt when your mom or dad described the differences between their lives and yours.

In *Night-Night* I suggest telling your child "Mommy stories"—stories of what life was like for you as a child, how you celebrated holidays, spent summers, and so on. My suggestion now? That you contrast your child's life, your life, and your mom's or dad's life. Surely you're enough aware of the circumstances of your mother's childhood that you could tell your child something like, "You play games on the computer and you spend part of the day watching TV but when I was a kid, we didn't have a computer, and when Grandma was a kid, she didn't even have a TV until she was eight years old." "Your older brother rides an electric scooter. When I was a kid I rode a Big Wheel—a kind of big, plastic tricycle. And when Grandma was a girl, she had a scooter like your brother's—except that it wasn't electric." "When I don't have time to cook dinner, I can pop a frozen dinner in the microwave. When I was a kid, my mom didn't have a microwave. She had to cook frozen dinners in the oven. And when Grandma was a kid, there were very few frozen dinners available . . . and most of them tasted yucky-gross-blecccccchhh."

If he wants, he can ask questions about other aspects of life and how they differed from Grandma's childhood to your childhood to his.

Relaxing Story
Activities

31

Mom's Day...as a Child

Besides describing what Christmas, summers, birthday parties, and other special times were like in your childhood, and besides contrasting aspects of life for your child, you as a child, and Grandma as a child, you can also describe an average day for you when you were your child's age or any age when you were a child.

If your child is three or four, what was a typical day like for you when *you* were three or four? In particular, emphasize the ways in which it differed from her life. Did you go to pre-school or daycare or Head Start? Did you stay home with your mom or dad or a babysitter? What time did you get up in the morning? Did you get to sleep as late as you wanted or were you woken up at a certain time so you wouldn't be late? Were you allowed to dress yourself or did you wear what your mom picked out for you? What did you usually have for breakfast? If you went to pre-school, did your dad pack your lunch? What did you usually have in your lunch? What did you do at pre-school? How did you get there? Did your mom or dad walk you, drive you, or send you on a schoolbus or in a carpool?

If you stayed home, what did you usually do? Did your dad play games with you? What games? What boxed games did you have? Any of the same ones your child has? Did your mom read to you? What were your favorite books and stories? What games did you like to play when you were home with your dad? Did you play hide and seek? What were your favorite hiding places? Did you play outdoors? Did your house have a backyard? What was the backyard like? Did you have a swing set or croquet game or other backyard equipment?

Did you and your mom often do errands and shopping together? What was your favorite store to visit? Why was it your favorite? Did any of the store owners give you candy or fruit or other goodies? Was there a mechanical horse or merry-go-round to ride outside the store? Did you ever shoplift or do anything else bad at any of the stores? How did your parents find out? What did they tell you? What did they do to you? What did you do to make things right between you and the store owner?

Was your mom a good cook? Your dad? What was your favorite dinner? What was your least favorite dinner? What did your mom do when you didn't like the dinner she served? Did she make you eat it anyhow? Make you taste it? Or cook something else for you? What was your favorite dessert?

Did you bathe at night or in the morning? What was your favorite bath toy? Did you have a special bath routine? Did it involve singing a special bath song like "Rubber Ducky"? After your bath, did your mom wrap you in a big, fluffy towel? Did you go straight to bed after that?

Who put you to bed at night? Mom? Dad? Both of them on different nights? Did they read you a story, tell you a story, play a game, or just kiss you good-night?

What else was a part of your days? Did you live near the firehouse and watch the engines go past? Did you have a bird's nest in the tree outside your window or did squirrels live in the tree? Was there a rabbit or woodchuck living in your yard? Did you live near an airport and watch planes all through the day? Did you sometimes drive to the airport just to watch the planes take off and land?

Tell your child the intricate details that made up the warp and woof of the everydays of your childhood.

Mr. Moose's Day

Actually it doesn't have to be a moose. Any animal will do. Just ask your child to tell you about an animal's day. The animal could be a bunny, a horse, your pet cat or your child's turtle, or even a dragon or dinosaur if your child has an active imagination. All your child has to do for this story activity is imagine what the animal he chooses does all day, and describe that day from the time the animal wakes up in the morning until the time it goes to sleep at night. That's all. But it's enough. Enjoy it.

Family History Lesson

This activity may teach a lesson—something about your child's family history; but it's still a story—the story of your family. In fact, it's many stories. Does your child know where Grandma and Grandpa met? Or how her other-side-of-the family grandparents met? Does she know what different countries her ancestors came from (or how many generations back)? Does she know that Grandpa Bob used to be a baker, Grandma Marie raised nine children plus two foster children, Pop Alan flew planes in the Air Force, Nan-Nan Joyce won awards for her pies and cakes, and her great-great-great-great-grandpa was the mayor of a small village in Poland?

Tell her those family stories that would interest her at greater length as well as a compilation of tidbits in cases where either you don't know more than the bare facts or the details would not hold her interest. Don't be surprised if she has trouble remembering who's who on the family tree (see Oral Family Tree, page 97). For now, it's enough that she knows some of the stories—and that she gets lulled to sleep by them. She can get straight on which great-grandpa was married to Great-Grandma Sophie when she gets older.

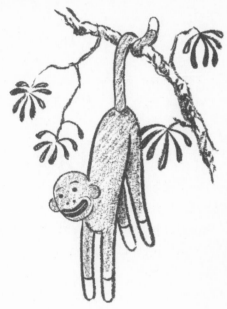

Games and Activities That Promote Relaxation

Some games are clearly unsuitable for pre-naptime. You wouldn't suggest that your child race around the yard in a wild chase game just before trying to lie down and sleep. You wouldn't even want her to get mentally or emotionally revved up. But the idea of a "game" doesn't have to equate with "excitement" or "stimulation." Some games and other activities are at least calm if not downright soothing; they're perfectly suitable for engaging in before attempting sleep.

Games can divert your child from thoughts that might get in the way of her getting to sleep. They can put her in a happy, contented state of mind, allowing her to drift off more easily.

Here are some games and other activities that may help your child settle down and get ready to sleep. In this section you'll also find a few "special treats" that may help your child look forward to naptime as an adventure instead of something to resist.

# Do As I Do

This one's a bit of a trick that will only work once—though you can make up variations on it and even suggest to your child that, as she lies there waiting to go to sleep, *she* can think of variations herself.

Here's what you do: You and the child both sit facing each other. You say, "Watch me and then do *exactly* what I did." Hold your left hand upright with the palm facing you and the fingers spread out. Put the index finger of your right hand on your left pinkie finger and say, "Johnny." Now touch your ring finger and say, "Johnny." Middle finger. "Johnny." Index finger. "Johnny." Now slide your right index finger along from the tip of your left index finger down into the "valley" between it and your thumb, and back up again along the inside of your thumb to the tip of your thumb. As you do this, say, "Whooooops." Now touch the tip of your thumb and say, "Johnny." Now slide the opposite way, from your thumbtip back down and up again to the tip of your index finger, again saying, "Whooooops." And touch each of your four fingers in turn again, from index back to pinkie, saying, "Johnny," each time you touch a fingertip.

Important: When you are finished, clasp your hands in your lap.

Now say, "Can you do that?"

On the first few tries, your child will probably get some part of the basic maneuver wrong. She may leave out a "Johnny" or get the "Whooooops" part wrong. *Do not correct her when she makes the mistake. Do not tell her where she goofed up. Let her get all the way through the procedure.* Then, when she finishes and says, "Was I right?" say, "No. Watch me, I'll do it again." And demonstrate again. Eventually she'll get it all correct—but it's unlikely that she'll realize that clasping her hands in her lap at the end is intrinsic to getting it right. At some point she'll catch on—or she'll give up and you'll tell her. If she starts getting frustrated, give her hints—even strong hints if need be.

If she gets upset, which is not conducive to sleepiness, you can soothe her quickly by pointing out the fun she's going to have playing this trick on her friends.

Variations: You can make up variations on this game, such as using your *left* index finger on your *right* hand, or stopping to scratch your cheek in the middle of the game. Or make up a whole new routine altogether. Then suggest to her that *she* make up one of these to trick *you* with.

Counting Squirrels

Even if your child doesn't know his numbers well, he can picture *one* squirrel and then picture it side by side with *another* squirrel and then *another* squirrel and *another* squirrel. But if he *does* know his numbers, he can count *one, two, three, four, five* and so on till he can no longer see that many squirrels or he gets to a number higher than he can count to . . . or falls asleep.

This is a cross between "counting sheep" and practicing counting.

A Walk Around the Block

If you live on a suburban or city block and your child has been around the block with you on foot (or on a wheeled toy of some sort), do this as "A Walk Around the Block." If she knows only your street, or if you live in a cul-de-sac or on a long rural road, play it as "A Walk up the Street."

Ask her to pretend she's setting out from your front door for a walk around the block. Ask her to imagine she's walking out the front door of your house or apartment building and to describe everything she sees.

Though this is supposed to be an exercise in recalling things observed, don't criticize if she turns it into a flight of fancy. If she starts describing polka-dotted flowers and twenty-foot hedges that don't exist, you can chuckle and say, "That would be quite a sight, wouldn't it?!", reminding her that her descriptions aren't reality yet acknowledging that you respect her right to fantasize.

If, on the other hand, she skimps on the details and says only, "The Thompsons' house is next door, and then there's another house. . . ." prompt her for details: "What

Games and
Activities That
Promote
Relaxation

43

color is the Thompsons' house? What does it look like? What kind of fence or hedge do they have out front? Do they have a tree in the yard?" and other appropriate questions.

If she doesn't know, don't criticize her or press her. Just say, "Well, next time we go for a walk, we'll have to look more carefully, okay?" If there are other details you think she might be aware of, ask her, "Is there a tree next to the curb near the Thompsons' house? Is it a big tree? Does it have acorns?"

When she's gotten to the corner in her imaginary walk, kiss her and tell her to have a good nap, and suggest that until she falls asleep, she should keep walking around the block in her imagination trying to "see" all the houses she can in her mind and all the details she can think of about each. Or, if she doesn't know the whole block, suggest that she walk back toward your house from the corner and "see" all the details she can including as many as possible that she missed while "walking away from home." Or have her leave your house and turn in the opposite direction so that this time she turns left instead of right when she gets to the sidewalk.

Tongue Twisters

How many times can your child repeat these phrases before his tongue gets "twisted" and the words come out wrong? How many times can *you* say them correctly? Let him laugh at your efforts, too!

Three free eels freeze.

Summer soups are simply super.

Pick a tricky trio of treetops.

Treetops twist and twirl in the gale.

Snails and slugs are simply silly.

Little Lizzie lit a large light.

Circus Game

This simple pastime involves saying a poem while doing finger and hand motions. Here is the poem with my suggested finger motions, though you're certainly free to use different ones if you prefer.

Up the hill and down,
> [*Walk your fingers up your child's body and down*]

The kids are all yelling
> [*Touch her mouth*]

And everyone's telling:
> [*Touch her mouth again*]

The circus has come to town!
> [*Clap your hands against hers once*]

See the silly clown!
> [*Spread the corners of her mouth into a silly smile*]

He's stumbling and bumbling
> [*Shake her legs*]

And tripping and tumbling.
> [*Tumble your hands across her belly*]

The circus has come to town!
> [*Clap your hands against hers once*]

Popsicle Puppets

You can prepare these puppets ahead of time or, if you want to, you can have your child help you make them. All you need is two Popsicle sticks, two circles cut out of construction paper, some crayons or marking pens, and glue or paste.

The circles are the puppets' faces. Using crayon or marking pen, draw smiles and/or wide eyes or whatever you think will appeal to your child. Still working with the crayon or marking pen, give the puppets hair, eyebrows, noses, even ears—whatever works. Then paste each circle to the top of a Popsicle stick. This is the part you need to prepare in advance.

Now, at naptime, engage the puppets in conversation. The puppets can simply talk between themselves or can talk to your child. They can talk about anything you want or they can wish your child a good nap.

Here's a sample conversation:

ARTHUR (PUPPET #1): Hmmmm. It's time for a nap. Don't you think?

MARTHA (PUPPET #2): Yes. I always get sleepy around this time.

ARTHUR: Taking a nap helps me feel more energetic
later on.

MARTHA: Yes, if I nap I can play harder and have
more fun.

ARTHUR: What do you want to dream about?

MARTHA: Well, I'm going to think about nice things
till I fall asleep, so I have nice dreams while I'm
napping.

ARTHUR: Like what?

MARTHA: Well, I think I'll imagine that I'm floating on
a cloud and going around the world on it, and
seeing all kinds of things from up on top of my soft,
white, fluffy, comfortable cloud. What about you?

ARTHUR: I think I want to imagine myself digging
tunnels under the earth and coming up out of the
ground in new and exciting places.

MARTHA: Well, that sounds nice, but I think I'd rather
imagine my cloud can take me all the way to the
moon. What do you suppose the moon looks like
from up close?

ARTHUR: I don't know. But it would be fun to go there
and find out. And maybe to some of the planets out
there, too.

MARTHA: And I bet it would be fun to dig under the earth like you were talking about, too. I wonder if I would come up in Australia? Or the North Pole? Or maybe Asia?

ARTHUR: The North Pole? Do you think you'd see Santa Claus?

MARTHA: Maybe! Let's go!

ARTHUR: Okay! And then we'll go up to the moon or Mars next.

MARTHA: All right! Let's get ready.

ARTHUR: And even if we don't get there, we can dream about it!

MARTHA (to your child): Have nice dreams. Maybe *you'll* get to the moon too . . . at least in your dreams. (She "kisses" your child.)

ARTHUR (to your child): Or under the earth. You might get to lots of different places. Enjoy dreaming about it! (He "kisses" your child.)

Paper Plate Puppets

Still another form of puppet is the paper plate puppet. These are really nothing but faces drawn on the backs of paper plates. (Simple, inexpensive white plates work fine here.) If you want to get fancy, you can glue yarn hair in yellow, brown, black, or red to the tops of the plates, also gluing it down along the sides until it falls free from the widest part of the plate (or you can cut it off at the widest point for short hair). You can also glue cotton to make a white-haired great-grandma or older neighbor type.

But the hair isn't necessary. What's necessary is faces, and all you need for that is crayon or markers. In a pinch, you could even just draw faces with ink. Draw a face on the back of one paper plate and another on the back of another paper plate, trying to make the two look different, whether by eye color, mouth size, cheek coloring, or other distinguishing characteristics.

Now hold one plate in each hand and simply have the two faces talk to each other and to your child. You can use the dialogue suggested in the previous Popsicle Puppets game or simply ad lib a conversation. Here's another script you can use if you want:

LEE (PUPPET # 1): Gee, I'm sleepy.

PAT (PUPPET # 2): Why don't you take a nap?

LEE: Because I really wanted to talk to Alan, here.

PAT: Alan's going to take a nap too.

LEE: How about I talk to Alan for just a few minutes? Alan, what's your favorite food? (Ad lib a conversation about food, candy, fire trucks, anything.)

PAT: Alan, Lee's tired. Let's let Lee get a nap. You two can talk some more tomorrow. A person who's tired really should get some sleep. In fact, it's a good idea to take a nap every day even if you don't feel tired. It gives you lots more energy and strength for the rest of the day.

Coin Toss Game

In its most elemental form, the game consists simply of tossing a coin while your child predicts "Heads" or "Tails" in the usual manner. How often will he be right? He shouldn't get too worked up over winning (or losing), so it's a suitable game to play before a nap, one that won't get him revved.

If you want to give the game more interest, you'll need nine (or some other odd number of your choosing) pennies. Explain that you'll toss the coin nine times (or as many times as the number of pennies you're playing with), and if he guesses heads or tails right, he gets a penny, but if he guesses wrong, you get the penny. When you've tossed the coin nine times, and distributed all nine pennies, if he has more pennies than you, he's won the game, but if you have more pennies, he didn't win. (It's nicer to put it that way than "You've lost" or even "I've won"—it's not a contest between you and him.)

Instead of pennies, you can use checkers or scraps of paper or even paper clips.

You don't need to play for prizes—the fun of winning is reward enough, though if you'd like, you can certainly promise a modest prize to him if he wins. Prizes might include all nine pennies for his piggy bank, an extra cookie when it's time for milk and cookies, a second story at bedtime, or some other minimal privilege.

Suggestion: For kids who are too little to count and would have trouble discerning whether they have won or not, you can take one penny (or checker or whatever) from you and one from him, and push them aside. Then take another from you and another from him, and push them aside. Continue till one of you has no pennies or checkers left. This will make it obvious whether he won or not, even if he can't count.

Where Is Teddy Hiding?

Your child can play this variation on Hide 'n' Seek with you without ever leaving her bed. Here's how:

Have her imagine a hiding place for her teddy bear somewhere in her room. It doesn't have to be a place her bear could actually fit into. It could be under the bed, in her closet, in the wastebasket, in a dresser drawer, in her toy chest, in a night table drawer or . . . well, I don't know the geography of your child's room. But you do, and she does.

She picks out a place in her mind to "hide Teddy," after which you have to "find him." You can ask the obvious questions first: Is he under the covers? Is he in the closet? Is he in the toy chest? If you strike out in several such guesses, you can ask other questions to narrow down which side of the room she's hidden him on, whether he's up high or down low, whether he's inside something or behind furniture, and any other questions that will help you.

She's honor bound not to change his hiding place in mid-round; but of course, once you've found him, she can hide him all over again for another round, if you want.

Horsefeathers!

We all know the common word for something that isn't true—it begins with "bull" and ends with a four-letter word you don't want your children using. For that matter, you don't want them saying "That's a lie!" either. There are many acceptable expressions, of course, including the venerable "Horsefeathers," which presumably derives from the fact that there is no such thing as "horsefeathers."

Challenge your child to come up with a few similar expressions, such as "cat antlers" or "snake wings" or "mouse horns" or "whale feet." How many can he think of? It doesn't matter how silly they are—as long as they're not offensive, they can become your family's pet words to deride the veracity of a statement. And even if you never use them for that, thinking of them will make him feel silly and giggly and put him in a good condition for drifting off for his nap.

Games and
Activities That
Promote
Relaxation

Challenging Mommy

Well, this isn't really much of a challenge for you but your child will enjoy putting you in the hot seat (or thinking she's doing so); and the best part is, she can learn something in the process.

If your pint-size child is still learning such basic concepts as "under," "over," and "near," or her colors, or "large" and "small," or any similar concepts, you probably ask her periodically if she can point to something green or tell you what's *on* the chair or *under* the table. Now it's her turn to challenge you—and she'll still learn in the process.

Have her offer you similar challenges—to find something in her room that's blue or to touch something that's on top of something else. And, of course, when you correctly point to something appropriate, she'll still be learning the appropriate meaning and use of these classifications.

Simplified Scavenger Hunt

For this game, your child needs to be old enough to mentally picture different parts of the house and to figure out just what objects you're describing. But you can make the descriptions easier or tougher, according to your child's ability. What you're going to do is describe an object without naming it; your child then needs to tell you where that object is found.

An obvious and easy example for a very young player would be: "It has pictures on the screen. We watch it and listen to it. We watch shows and movies on it."

The child, recognizing that you're describing the family's TV set, needs only to say, "It's in the living room." Or the family room, or wherever your TV is located.

For just a little more difficult challenge offer "We use these to eat with. They carry food from our plates to our mouths." He probably knows that you're talking about utensils. Even if he doesn't know that word, he can say "spoons and forks," or you may call it "silverware" even if it isn't literally silver. And he can probably tell you that they're found in a kitchen drawer. Or on the table. Or, if your family is like many I know, they're often in the dishwasher.

Now try describing the phone, one of his toys, his socks, the milk container, and whatever other familiar objects you think he can recognize from your description and correctly describe the usual location of.

That Makes Sense(s)

Help your child become more aware of the five senses while you help her relax and fall asleep for her nap. Ask her what her favorite thing is to see or look at. Don't be disappointed if she says "TV" instead of "the sunset." Now ask her what her favorite sound is. The other three questions are: What feels especially good when you touch it? What do you especially love to smell? What do you most love to taste?

Now ask her what her *least* favorite sight, sound, smell, taste, and touch are.

Next—or another day—you can ask her for *other* favorites besides the five she's already listed. What *else* feels especially good to touch, tastes really, really, really good, looks very pretty, sounds particularly nice, and smells really good?

This Is the Church, This Is the Steeple. . . .

This is a very simple (and very old) amusement for the very young set. To start, fold your fingers down and put your two hands together so that your fingers interlock at the knuckles and your right index finger is alongside your left index finger, your right middle finger is alongside your left middle finger, and so on. Your two thumbs should be straight, sticking upward, and side by side. As you put your hands in this position, say, "This is the church."

Now unfold your two index fingers so they point upward and touch each other, finger pad to finger pad. As you do this, say, "This is the steeple."

Now separate your two thumbs, holding them wide apart, and say, "Open the door."

Last, turn your hands so that, with the fingers still inter-locked, the backs of your hands are touching each other. Straighten your fingers up. The last line, which accompanies this move, is "And see all the people."

It may seem pretty much of a nothing to you, but it amuses the heck out of a two-year-old.

Where Is Thumbkin?

Also amusing to a little kid and probably just as old as "This Is the Church" is this song-game. The tune is the same as "Frère Jacques."

With your hands in fists and behind your back, sing, "Where is thumbkin? Where is thumbkin?"

Pull one hand out from behind your back with just the thumb sticking out and wiggle it, singing, "Here I am."

Then repeat with the other hand, singing, "Here I am."

Wiggle the thumb on one hand and sing, "How are you this morning?"

Wiggle the other thumb and sing, "Very well, I thank you."

Put one hand behind your back as you sing, "Run away."

Then the other hand goes behind your back as you repeat, "Run away."

For the next verse, you do the same thing, except that you extend and wiggle your index finger. The words are "Where is pointer?"

The remaining verses are "Where is tall man?" "Where is ring man?" and "Where is pinkie?"

When the two pinkies have "run away," the game is over. Of course, you can sing it again and suggest that this time your child do the finger motions with you. (Play the game often enough and she'll soon be singing along with you.)

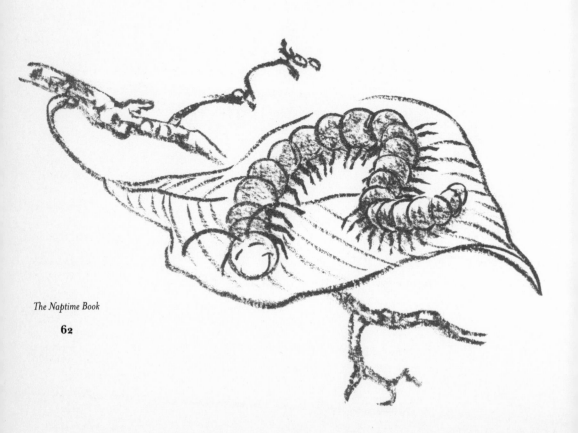

Insect Parade

All there is to this silly little game is some finger motions
and a poem. Let your right hand tickle its way up your
child's arm at a moderate rate during the first three lines
of the poem. Then, for the last line, bring your left hand
into play and scurry it quickly up her arm (the same arm or
the other one), so that it reaches her chin as you finish
talking. Tickle her chin for a second . . . and you're done.

Here's the poem:

> The spider scurried up the street.
> He moved real fast with all those feet.
> But even faster, yes indeed,
> Was his new friend, the centipede!

Games and
Activities That
Promote
Relaxation

I Spy...With My Eyes Closed

In the old familiar game, "I Spy," one person says, "I spy, with my little eye, something that begins with ____ [letter of the alphabet]." The guesser then has to guess what it is. In this version, since you're playing with a child whom you want to have go to sleep, he'll keep his eyes closed instead of looking around. Since he's not yet a speller, your clue will be nonalphabetic. And since you *want* him to win, your clue will be rather broad so it will be easy for him to guess without getting frustrated.

In fact, you can give him several clues, either one at a time or all at once. Just how easy you make the game will depend on your child's age, how good he is at envisioning things in his mind, and what his frustration tolerance level is.

While he lies on the bed with his eyes closed, you look around his room. Perhaps you will choose his toy chest, wooden and painted to look like a circus train car. You might say, "I spy something large and made of wood."

He guesses, "My bookcase?"

You say, "No, it holds things but not books."

He guesses, "My toy chest?"

You tell him he's right, and you choose something else and play again.

For a harder item to guess, you can give more information with your "I spy" sentence such as "I spy something blue that's all over the room and feels warm and fuzzy." (It's his carpet.) For an older child, on the other hand, you can make the clues harder. And for a change of pace, he can be the one to "spy" something while you guess what it is, but generally you want to spy while he lies there, picturing his room in his mind . . . with his eyes shut.

Our Next Guest ... *Version 1*

For this you'll probably want an empty cardboard tube from a roll of toilet paper or paper towels, or you could use a wooden spoon or something similar. It's not essential, but it helps. Your child pretends to be a radio or TV interviewer or news reporter who's interviewing you. You play the part of yourself (now, isn't that easy?!).

The "interviewer" holds the "microphone" out to you and asks you questions. You answer them. Depending on your child's age and interests, these may be silly questions, questions about what you did today or questions about what's for dinner.

What's really good is if you can steer her to asking you questions about the family—family history, your childhood, or family stories. As you answer, she gains some insight into her family, their background, and their true stories of the past, making for a better understanding of her family and her own background.

Our Next Guest . . . *Version 2*

Play this game similarly to the previous one but now instead of your being yourself, you pretend to be someone else. Let your child guide you as to who you are, when he says, "Our next guest is ____." You now have to answer the questions as the person you're supposed to be. You might be called upon to be a real person though more likely he'll want you to be a "type"—a scientist, a police officer, a movie star, perhaps a zookeeper.

Then you take a turn being the interviewer and he's the interviewee. Now he has to pretend to be a lion-tamer, clown, famous writer, football player, or space traveler.

Unlike the previous version of this game, this version won't increase his knowledge of family history . . . but it's great for stretching his "imagination muscles." And it's a good lure to get him on the bed for his nap.

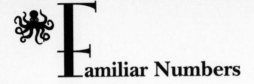

Familiar Numbers

Does your child know a familiar number when she "meets" one? If you say "Four," will she reply "My age!"? If you say "Twenty-nine," will she recognize it as your house number? If you've taught her to dial "9-1-1" in an emergency, will she recognize the number if you say it aloud? Does she know that "seven" is her older brother's age? That "thirty-two" is the corner you're on—the corner of 32nd Street? That "555-2856" is your phone number? That "twelve" is the floor Great-Gran Rhonda lives on in her apartment building?

Test her—and make a game of it.

"A Blue Sky to Fly In"

On a similar principle to the old standard "This Is the House That Jack Built," "A Blue Sky to Fly In" builds line upon line, verse upon verse, and challenges your ability to remember the entire rhyme.

In fact, your child and even you may have trouble remembering it all even after many repetitions, so until you've got it down by heart, go ahead and read it and coach him along as he learns more and more of the rhyme each time you say it together.

To make it even more fun for him, you can make appropriate hand motions in the air, with your hand zooming or floating or gracefully flying as you read the rhyme (or perhaps eventually even learn to say it by heart). There is no prescribed set of motions; just use your imagination and let your hand do what the words say. There's no right and wrong motions here, and if your robin and your bat look similar, no problem.

Ready? Here's the rhyme:

Here's a blue sky to fly in.
Here's a robin up in the sky, the pretty blue sky to fly in.
Here's a kite that's bobbing up high. It flies past the
    robin up in the sky, the pretty blue sky to fly in.
Here's a plane that's flying right by. It flies by the kite
    that's bobbing up high, that flies past the robin up
    in the sky, the pretty blue sky to fly in.
There's the pilot, yelling, "Oh, my!" He pilots the plane
    that's flying right by, that flies by the kite that's
    bobbing up high, that flies past the robin up in the
    sky, the pretty blue sky to fly in.

The co-pilot looks him right in the eye, right at the pilot
who's yelling, "Oh, my!" He pilots the plane that's
flying right by. It flies by the kite that's bobbing up
high, that flies past the robin up in the sky, the
pretty blue sky to fly in.

A bat is flying—this is no lie. The bat sees the co-pilot
look in the eye, the eye of the pilot who's yelling,
"Oh, my!" He pilots the plane that's flying right by.
It flies by the kite that's bobbing up high, that flies
past the robin up in the sky, the pretty blue sky to
fly in.

And there's a cloud. It's white and quite dry. It floats
past the bat—and this is no lie. The bat sees the
co-pilot look in the eye, the eye of the pilot who's
yelling, "Oh, my!" He pilots the plane that's flying
right by. It flies by the kite that's bobbing up high,
that flies past the robin up in the sky, the pretty
blue sky to fly in.

A parachutist—what a brave guy!—jumps out of a
'copter and doesn't once cry. He jumps through the
cloud that's white and quite dry, which floats past
the bat—and this is no lie. The bat sees the co-pilot
look in the eye, the eye of the pilot who's yelling,
"Oh, my!" He pilots the plane that's flying right by.

It flies by the kite that's bobbing up high, that flies past the robin up in the sky, the pretty blue sky to fly in.

The sun is shining ever so high. It shines on the para-chutist—brave guy—who jumps from the 'copter and doesn't once cry. He jumps through the cloud that's white and quite dry, which floats past the bat—and this is no lie. The bat sees the co-pilot look in the eye, the eye of the pilot who's yelling, "Oh, my!" He pilots the plane that's flying right by. It flies by the kite that's bobbing up high, that flies past the robin up in the sky, the pretty blue sky to fly in.

This story's long, and I'll tell you why. When I tell a story, I am not shy. I'll talk of the sun that's shining so high. It shines on the parachutist—brave guy—who jumps from the 'copter and doesn't once cry. He jumps through the cloud that's white and quite dry, which floats past the bat—and this is no lie. The bat sees the co-pilot look in the eye, the eye of the pilot who's yelling, "Oh, my!" He pilots the plane that's flying right by. It flies by the kite that's bobbing up high, that flies past the robin up in the sky, the pretty blue sky to fly in.

It's in the Bag! – *Version 1*

In this easier version of the game (see the next game for a harder version), you show your child five or six objects that are small enough to fit in a brown paper bag (or other bag that can't be seen through). Then you turn your back so she can't see what you're doing. Now you put one of the objects in the bag and the remainder of the objects in another bag, so she can't see which one is missing.

Offer her the bag with the one object in it. She sticks her hand in and feels it, taking as much time as she wants to hold it, examine it by touch, and try to determine which it is of the five or six objects you showed her. She may not, of course, take it out and look at it.

Then she guesses and you tell her if she's right or wrong.

You can limit her to one guess or let her keep at it until she's got it right, if only by process of elimination.

Obviously the objects need to be small enough to fit in the bag and not too similar to each other. You don't want two buttons, two different coins, or two items that are of different sorts but would feel substantially similar. You are not trying to trick her; you want her to win.

It's in the Bag! — *Version 2*

Similar to the game that preceded this one, this is a more
challenging version for your older napper. In this version,
you don't show the child five or six objects first. You merely
select one object, put it in a paper bag or other bag that
can't be seen through, and then have the child feel it until
he thinks he knows what it is.

You need to select an item that he's pretty well familiar
with, nothing too esoteric, nothing he can't readily identify.

If you wish, you can give hints, either one at a time
or even several at a time: "I use it in the kitchen. I keep it
in the drawer next to the stove. I use it to stir when I'm
cooking."

If the child doesn't know the right name for an object
but can still describe it in such a way that you know
he knows what he's holding inside the bag, that's good
enough. This isn't a vocabulary game.

What's Missing?

Writing up the first version of "It's in the Bag" made me remember this old favorite that bears a minimal similarity to it. For this game, you need a tray, platter, or other large flat surface and five or six small objects (such as a thimble, a coin, a button, a paper clip, and an eraser). They should all be familiar objects the child can readily identify. (It's all right if, for instance, she doesn't know that the coin is a dime, as long as she can say "It's money.")

Arrange all the objects on the tray and let your child study them. Then leave the room, remove one of the objects from the tray, and return to the room. Can your child tell you which object is missing? You can leave a space where you took out the one item or you can close up the space but don't rearrange the placement.

If she gets very good at this game, you can make it more difficult for her as follows: When you remove the one object from the tray, rearrange the order in which you have the others. Now it will be harder for her to ascertain what's missing.

Presto-Change-o

If your child enjoys playing "What's Missing" (see page 75), she may also enjoy this related game. Ages old, it goes by various names but the premise is always the same: You leave the room and change one thing about your appearance. You might put on or take off a pair of glasses, pull your hair up into a bun or ponytail or let it down from one so it hangs loose, put on or take off a sweater, put a handkerchief into your pocket so it sticks out visibly or remove one that was there, put on or take off your shoes, or do something else noticeable. If playing with an older child, you can try a more subtle difference such as unbuttoning one button.

When you return to the room, your child has to study you and figure out what's different. (It's okay to give her hints if she gets stuck.)

Circle, Square, Rectangle, Triangle

For the child who has learned to recognize shapes when he sees them, and to name them, this game can be great fun as he proves how much he knows.

Ask him to look around his room as he lies in bed and find something that's circle-shaped—a ball, the doorknob. Now what can he see that's square? Depending on what's in your child's room, this might include a tabletop or a box or a window. Many things in his room are probably rectangles, including the bed he's lying on! Probably his dresser, the doors to his room and his closet, and his toy chest are among the other examples of rectangular objects in his room. Surely he has some rectangular books!

Triangles will be the hardest. If you don't see any examples of triangles in his room, you can ask him, "Do you see any triangles?" and then praise him if he can't find any, saying, "Good. You didn't make a mistake. There aren't any."

If he's a bit older, you can ask him to mentally picture the rest of the house and think of all the examples he can of the different shapes. For this slightly older child you can also add "oval" to the mix of shapes you want him to think of examples of.

# Magic Trick

What kid won't get ready for a nap quickly if you promise to show him a magic trick when he gets there? Here's the trick—and indeed "trick" is the key operative word, for, as with all magic tricks, there's indeed a trick to performing it.

Tell him that you can "feel" colors and will tell him what color crayon he has put in a paper bag by just sticking your hand in and feeling the crayon. Turn your back, leave the room, or go into his closet—anything to show that you're not peeking. While you're not looking, he chooses one crayon from his crayon box and puts it in a paper bag that you've provided. While he watches (so he can see that you're not peeking into the bag), you stick your hand in and feel the crayon so you can tell what color it is—or at least, that's what you say you're doing.

What he doesn't know is that what you're actually doing is scraping it with a fingernail and getting a bit of the crayon under the nail.

When you take your hand out of the bag, you wave the

hand around and make a big deal about the vibrations that are coming through your fingers, the color waves that are shooting up to your eyes, the messages that your hand is sending to your brain . . . but what you're really doing is checking under your fingernails to see what color crayon wax you've scraped off.

You don't need to know the exact name of the color. "Brown" or "light purple" or "red" is close enough. Chances are he can't read and doesn't yet know the official crayon color names anyhow. And of course, you will get it right—to your child's amazement!

Just do the trick once. Then tuck him in for his nap. If he wants you to repeat the trick, promise that you will—tomorrow, just before he takes his nap. There's incentive to get him in for his nap tomorrow! Although, if he wants to try to do it himself, you can let him have two tries (tell him in advance that's all he gets) before you tuck him in, take the bag out of the room (remove the temptation!), and leave him to nap.

Games and
Activities That
Promote
Relaxation

Naptime for Mommy?

One woman I know on occasion got her child to nap by asking her daughter to put *her* in for a nap. When the daughter tucked the mother in, the mother started a series of demands—a teddy bear, a drink of water, and so forth. At long last, after running the daughter ragged getting item after item, the mom closed her eyes and pretended to sleep. At that point, the daughter lay down next to her and went to sleep for real.

Once your child is soundly asleep, of course, you can get up again . . . but you might also want to take a nap that isn't pretend, and there's no reason not to nap snuggled up to your child. Just be careful not to make a regular occurrence out of it so that she refuses to nap unless you're sleeping next to her.

This Is the Way...

You know the song, "This is the way we ____"? Your child can get ready for his nap to that tune and make a little game out of the preparations getting himself in the right frame of mind at the same time. Sing it along with him, kiss him where the song indicates, and even fluff the pillow with him if you want:

> This is the way I/you fluff my/your pillow,
> Fluff my/your pillow,
> Fluff my/your pillow,
> This is the way I/you fluff my/your pillow,
> Before I/you take my/your nap.

> This is the way I/you take off my/your shoes,
> Take off my/your shoes,
> Take off my/your shoes,
> This is the way I/you take off my/your shoes,
> Before I/you take my/your nap.

This is the way I/you sit on the bed,
Sit on the bed,
Sit on the bed,
This is the way I/you sit on the bed,
Before I/you take my/your nap.

This is the way I/you pull up my/your quilt,
Pull up my/your quilt,
Pull up my/your quilt,
This is the way I/you pull up my/your quilt,
Before I/you take my/your nap.

This is the way that I kiss you,
I kiss you,
I kiss you,
This is the way that I kiss you,
Before I/you take my/your nap.

This is the way I/you close my/your eyes,
Close my/your eyes,
Close my/your eyes.
This is the way I/you close my/your eyes,
Before I/you take my/your nap.

And pretty soon I'll/you'll go to sleep,
Go to sleep,
Go to sleep,
And pretty soon I'll/you'll go to sleep,
When I/you take my/your nap.

And when I/you sleep I'll/you'll have nice dreams,
Have nice dreams,
Have nice dreams,
And when I/you sleep I'll/you'll have nice dreams.
When I/you take my/your nap.

Sleep-over Party

Tempt your child to nap by offering her a "sleep-over party" with her five (three, eight—whatever number will work in terms of space) favorite stuffed animals. If she's usually allowed to bring just one teddy bear, toy dog, doll, or whatever to bed with her, declare a holiday and a special exception, and call it a sleep-over party. Tell her she may—just this once—pick five stuffed "friends" to join her on the bed . . . providing she *and they* go right to sleep.

Tell her the animals have to nap too, and if she hears any talking, Mr. Bear or Patches the dog—whoever's doing the whispering—will have to leave the bed, as she and the animals all need their naps.

With this little bit of whimsy, settle her on the bed or tuck her under her nap quilt and kiss everyone "Good nap"—the animals as well as your child.

The Clapping Game

As you recite (or read) the poem below, your child can clap the appropriate parts of his body. (Until he gets the hang of it, you can help him along by clapping his hands, feet, etc. together.)

> Feel the rhythm. Feel the beat.
> Clap your hands. Now clap your feet.
> Next you'll use your doorbell ringers.
> Yes, I mean you clap your fingers.
> Feel real silly? Great! Here goes.
> We're almost done, so clap your toes.
> And last of all, clap your elbows!

Games and
Activities That
Promote
Relaxation

Flashlight Pictures

You probably remember how to make flashlight shadow pictures from your own childhood—but have you ever shown your child how to make a horse or dog or donkey or a butterfly? You need a darkened room, a strong beam of light like a flashlight, and your two hands.

For the horse/dog/donkey (they are all done the same way but different people interpret them differently), place the thumb of one hand with the tip touching the lower knuckle of the index finger and the thumb slightly bowed out (suggesting a mouth), the middle fingertip touching the top of the index finger between the two knuckles (suggesting an eye), and the other two fingers sticking up and spread apart (suggesting tall-standing ears).

For the butterfly, hold your two hands straight up, with the palms facing away from you, the four fingers of each hand held together, and the two thumbs interlocked, suggesting a butterfly's two big wings with a body in the middle.

In each case, hold your hand or hands in the beam of light and let it project the silhouette of the animal onto the wall. (You need the light shining against a flat surface, not curtains.) You can leave the flashlight on a surface at the same level as your hands or ask your child to hold it and shine it on your hands and then look at the wall.

Very occasionally, a very small child will find the images scary. This doesn't happen often, but if it does, take your hands away from the light beam quickly and move on to another activity after a reassuring hug.

How Many?

Here's a simple pastime for you and your child to play for a few minutes before you kiss her "Good nap" and settle her in. It's a brain challenge but an easy one. When she thinks of plenty of answers, she'll feel good about herself and drift off in a good frame of mind.

All you have to do is ask a question of this sort: "How many ___ can you think of?" Then let her answer . . . and help her along if she gets stuck. Here are some sample questions:

❋ How many boys' names can you think of?

❧ How many girls' names can you think of?

🜺 How many green things can you think of?

❋ How many kinds of animals can you think of?

❋ How many things that fly can you think of? (Hint: Rather than just saying, "Birds, insects, planes," and perhaps "Helicopters and blimps," she can answer with names of different kinds of birds and different kinds of insects.) Oh, of course, paper airplanes fly too!

How many words can you think of that begin with the letter A? Obviously most kids of napping age aren't spellers so this aspect of the game would work best for older nappers. For pre-spellers, try the next question.

How many words can you think of with a "sssssss" sound in them?

How many kinds of cars can you think of?

How many kinds of flowers can you think of?

How many relatives—members of our family, like aunts and uncles and cousins—can you think of the names of?

Games and
Activities That
Promote
Relaxation

89

Naptime for Teddy

Your child may well take one stuffed animal (or doll) to bed with her, both at night and when she naps but she probably can't fit all her stuffed animals in bed. Choose one who she *isn't* taking to bed with her and suggest she put that one to bed for *his* nap before she gets in bed herself.

Teddy (or whoever it is) needs his own bed or sleeping place. This could be a cardboard box, a doll crib, or even a spot on the floor with a blanket pulled up over him. Let your child put Teddy to bed for *his* nap, and then you put the child in for hers.

But don't let her insist on putting *all* her animals and dolls to bed; if she has a typical kid's menagerie, she'll still be doing it when it's her bedtime.

Travels Without a Passport

In the same category of special privileges for once in a while as "Sleepover Party" (see page 84), you can also allow your child to nap somewhere different once in a while. I don't just mean the sofa or your bed; surely you can be more creative than that.

How about under the dining room table? Under a card table that's been draped with a sheet to form an impromptu tent? In a sleeping bag in the den or family room? Look around your house to see what other opportunities would make safe places for a child to nap. Make her nap an adventure that she'll look forward to instead of resisting.

There's an Echo in This Room

For this game, your child is to say everything you say, in
the same order, and see how many words he can get right.
Don't try to trick him. Make it as easy for him as you can.
Start with a string of three words. Don't use big words.
Don't confuse him with rhyming words like "box, fox,
socks." Just pick three words, perhaps "Ball, hat, house,"
and then repeat them again: "Ball, hat, house." Then say,
"Do you remember? What were the words?"

   If he can get those three in order, add another one:
"Ball, hat, house, bed." Keep adding a word till he messes
up. Then start over with a new set of three words. Play for a
few minutes then kiss him "Good nap" and leave the room.

There's a Shadow in This Room

In this game, you're going to ask your child to repeat a set of motions, in the same order as you performed them, rather as he did with words in "There's an Echo in This Room" (see page 92). But unlike "Do as I Do" (see page 40), you're not trying to trick him. There's no secret motion. This is a straightforward memory game.

For the first round, start with two motions—perhaps patting your tummy and scratching your cheek. Repeat the sequence, then ask him to mimic it. If he copies you correctly, add a third motion—perhaps sticking out your tongue, scrunching up your eyes, rubbing your chin, scratching your ear, or clapping your hands. If he can repeat all three motions correctly, try him on four.

When he messes up, don't pounce on him. This isn't a case of win or lose. Rather, praise him for how well he did overall and offer him a chance to start over with a new sequence. Do this a few times and then tuck him in for his nap and leave the room.

ho Am I?

How quickly can your child guess who you are speaking as?
She should get most of these right away but if not, give her
a hint (or two) until she guesses.

"I visit once a year and bring you presents, but you
don't see me when I'm at your house." (Santa Claus)

"I visit once a year and bring you candy in baskets. I
hop." (Easter Bunny)

"If you smell smoke or see big flames, you might need
me to come and help. I ride a red truck and slide down
a pole to get to the truck." (Firefighter)

"I help keep you feeling well, even though sometimes
that means giving you shots." (Doctor)

"I check your teeth and make sure they're clean and don't have any cavities. I might ask you if you're remembering to brush your teeth right." (Dentist)

"I stay with you in the evening if your parents aren't home." (Babysitter)

"I help keep you safe. If you're in trouble or lost, you should look for me." (Police officer)

You can make up clues of a similar type for other people your child knows and would easily recognize from the clue, such as, "I live next door and like to bake cookies," or "I'm your mother's mother and I live nearby." Try to stick with easy ones; you don't want to frustrate your child. This is a feel-good game designed to put her in a good frame of mind when she guesses right, not a game in which you're trying to best her.

# A Colorful Story

Ask your child to pick a color. Now ask him to make up a story in which as many things are that color as possible. Be sure to tell him they don't have to be things that are normally that color. If he picks pink, the hero of his story can put on a pink shirt and pink shoes, comb his pink hair, and go out and climb a pink tree, sit under a tree with pink leaves, fly a pink airplane, or swim in a pink lake.

Don't worry if there isn't much plot (or even sense) to his story. It's an exercise in stretching his creativity and a chance for him to focus on something relaxing. He isn't being judged on literary merit.

Oral Family Tree

This isn't really a game; it's an activity. But kids love to be tested on their knowledge and show how smart they are which is the basis of what you'll be doing here. The other premise of this activity is that kids have trouble remembering which family member is related to them in what way.

This is particularly true in large families and in families that don't get together very often. If your child sees his Aunt Gloria and Uncle Stu fairly often, he can put a face with the name and probably remember that Uncle Stu is Daddy's brother and Aunt Gloria is his wife. But if your sister and brother and their families live in another part of the country—or even just a two-and-a-half-hour drive away— your child may see them infrequently and have trouble remembering who's who.

Too, in today's divided and recombined families, a child may have five or seven or even eight grandparents and other family members who are "related" by remarriage— such as Uncle Seth's second wife's children from her first marriage.

Whew! It took longer to explain the premise than it will to explain the activity. In a nutshell: Feed your child family facts—who's related to him and how. Then test him on his knowledge. Praise him when he remembers right. Correct him gently when he misremembers. Allow him to wander off-track with comments like, "I like Aunt Zoe's dog. He's so shaggy and friendly and licky." And don't be critical when he expresses opinions like, "Uncle Harry is mean. He teases me." Maybe he's right. Maybe you even need to talk to Uncle Harry privately.

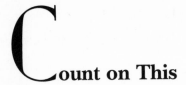

Count on This

Is your child old enough to know her numbers? Let her show off by counting aloud as she lies there. See how high she can go. Have her repeat it and see if she can get any higher this time. One more time? Okay, now let's try the alphabet. A - B - C. . . .

Color His World

With little ones who are still learning their colors, one quiet activity involves your mentioning familiar objects around the house and asking, "What color is it?" Describe each object and its location in enough detail that you can be sure your child is envisioning the correct thing: "You know the vase—the thing that I always put flowers in—that sits on the coffee table, next to the fruit bowl? Do you know what color it is?" "What about the bedspread that covers the bed in Daddy's and my bedroom? Can you tell me the two colors it is?" Try to avoid naming objects that are in colors such as mauve that he'd have trouble with, or that are more than two colors.

Silly, Soothing Poems

Instead of reading a story to your child, why not read him a few poems? In this section, you'll find some silly poems that may inspire mental pictures in your child that he can focus on as he drifts off to sleep at naptime.

The Silly Orchestra

Nina, Nina
Plays the concertina.
Her friend Tina
Plays the ocarina.
Lizzie, Tina's twin,
Plays the violin.
Ruth plays viola
And the pianola.
Her friend Suzette
Plays the clarinet.
Listen to the rhythm
Of the drums playing with them.
The drummers are Brian
And his friend Ryan.
While Patty plays trombone
With a sound that's all her own.
But the sound could make a few sick
'Cause not one of them reads music.

Noisy Oyster

A noisy noise annoys an oyster.
This they say is true.
But if you were a noisy oyster
Would the clams mind you?

A Lion's Chasing Me

A, B, C,
A lion's chasing me.
D, E, F, G,
It's got me up a tree.
H, I, J, K,
How can I get away?
L, M, N,
It's gone away again.
O, P, Q, R,
I'll still run very far.
S, T, U,
Oh wait! I've lost my shoe!
V, W, X, Y,
If it catches me, I'll cry.
Z,
I'm free!

Silly, Soothing
Poems

Shrinking Powder

I found a jar of shrinking powder,
Just a little one.
"Oh, boy, oh, boy!" I laughed aloud.
"I'm going to have some fun!"

I sprinkled just a little of it
On my sister's hair.
She shrank so small we couldn't
Even tell that she was there.

I sprinkled just a little
On a great big dog, and then,
The next thing he had turned
Into a puppy once again.

I sprinkled shrinking powder
On a really tall oak tree.
It shrank and shrank until it was
No taller than my knee.

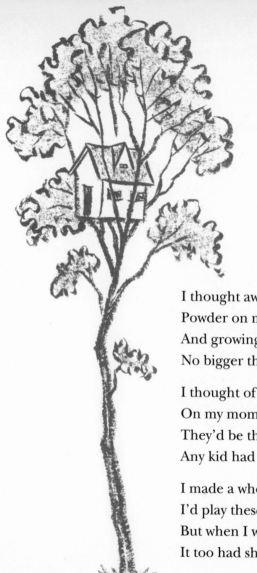

I thought awhile of sprinkling shrinking
Powder on myself,
And growing little 'til I was
No bigger than an elf.

I thought of sprinkling shrinking powder
On my mom and dad.
They'd be the smallest parents
Any kid had ever had.

I made a whole long list of whom
I'd play these tricks upon.
But when I went to find the jar,
It too had shrunk and gone.

The Fourth of July

Come out tonight, it's the Fourth of July.
Watch the fireworks light the sky.

Rockets blaze while the sparklers spark.
Roman candles light up the dark.

Firecrackers are all around.
Gee! They make such a startling sound!

Brilliant colors light up the sky.
Come and see! It's the Fourth of July!

Painting Animals

Tiger, tiger, in the zoo,
Who put those silly stripes on you?
Are they orange stripes on black,
Or black on orange, on your back?

The zebra's decorated too.
His pattern looks a lot like you.
But he got cheated, don't you think?
Just black and white . . . let's paint him pink!

Then while we're at it, would you say
The hippo's dull in solid gray?
Suppose we paint him bright chartreuse
And turn him loose with a purple moose?

Do elephants look good in blue?
Let's find out! By the time we're through,
There'll be a very different hue
To all the creatures in the zoo!

nna Banana

Anna Banana
Wore a red bandana
'Til a friendly clown
Gave her a gold crown.
And now though she's mean
She thinks she's a queen.

Yes, I Can!

By the time that I was two
I could put on my own shoe.
By the time that I was four
I could lock our front door.
And when I had got to six
I could play pick-up-sticks.
When I'd reached the age of eight
I could draw lines fairly straight.
And now that I am ten
I write neatly with a pen.
As I grow I can do more
Than I ever could before.

Silly, Soothing
Poems

109

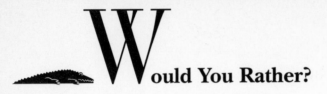# Would You Rather?

Would you rather be a lizard or a wizard?
Would you rather eat a cake or drink a lake?
Would you rather be a pilot or a pirate?
Or be a silly goose or a fake drake?

Would you like to walk through a busy crowd
Or wade through a puffy, fluffy cloud?

Would you rather be a heron or a herring,
Or a gnu in the zoo with the flu?
Let your imagination soar—
Go where you've never gone before.
And when you do, be really silly too!

Marian to the Moon

Marian was carryin'
Some blocks, some books, some belts.
She set up store outside her door.
Her plan was something else!

"I'll sell off every one of these things
And see what price each one of them brings.
Then I'll take my money
On a day that's sunny
And go and buy some wings.

"I'll fly to the moon
But I'd better go soon
Before it shrinks away.
It's disappearing fast
And I'm worried it won't last
For more than another day."

But the moon shrank very thin
Before she could begin
The trip she'd planned so well.

She sold her stuff for money
But it wasn't very funny.
What a sad, sad tale to tell.

The bright spot in this story
Is the moon returns to glory
Every month, so don't you pout.
And if Marian's wings fly,
Before a month goes by
She'll be on the moon, no doubt.

Alice from the Palace

Alice from the palace
Drinks from a golden chalice.
But she'd really rather sup
From her favorite plastic cup.

The Circus Comes to Town

Freddy is ready.
Freddy is excited.
Freddy just can't wait to see the clown.
Freddy's mom has tickets.
They're headed out the front door.
Today's the day the circus comes to town.

Of course there'll be horses,
Elephants and tigers,
Trapeze artists, high-wire walkers too.
Freddy's seat is front-row.
He'll see all the action.
Great big hoops with lions jumping through.

There's only one thing
That would make it better.
Freddy'd like to join the circus now.
Maybe one day, when
Freddy's gotten older
He'll be in that ring, taking his first bow.

Animal Goodbyes

"I'll see you later,"
Said the 'gator.
"I'm gonna wander,"
Said the salamander.
"I'm stepping out,"
Said the speckled trout.
"I'll be gone for a while,"
Said the crocodile.
"I'll be back again,"
Said the tiny wren.
"I've got to get bobbin',"
Said the red-breasted robin.
"I'm headed for that log,"
Said the wet green frog.
"I'm hitting the road,"
Said the dark brown toad.
"I'll be back, and that's that,"
Said the purring cat.
"Got to share a joke that's funny,"

And away hopped the bunny.
"I must get hopping too,"
Said the large kangaroo.
"I'm heading down the trail,"
Said the snail to the quail.
"Fly away with me,"
Said the fat striped bee.
And he started buzzin'
Round the wasp, his cousin.
"Good-bye. I'm out of here,"
Said the timid deer.
"I'm leaving. Good-bye,"
Said the butterfly.
Then the hungry moth
Fluttered off past the sloth.
Did anybody stay
When they all went away?
Yes—ugh!
A slug.

Silly, Soothing
Poems

115

Sounds

Trains go *Toot*
And owls go *Hoot,*
But what is the sound
Of an overripe fruit?
(*Squissssssshhhhh*)

Poor February! 🐱

The month of February
Really hasn't very
Many days to call its own.
The month of February
Can't feel very merry,
Seeing how it's all alone.

The other months all reach
At least thirty days each.
But February got left out.
Would it like some more
Days to keep in store?
Yes it would, without a doubt!

Maybe if we plead,
Telling of its need,
Other months would gladly share.
Surely they could find
A day they wouldn't mind
To give poor February as a spare.

But if they each gave one,
When they all were done,
The second month would have too many.
So what are we to do?
I haven't got a clue.
Not one idea. Have you got any?

Silly, Soothing
Poems

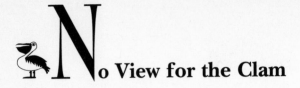# No View for the Clam

The clam has no windows to look out by day
And see if the oysters are coming to play.
The clam has no windows to look out at night.
To see if it's cloudy or moon-shiny bright.
The clam, with no windows, needs no drapes or blinds.
But somehow I don't think the little clam minds.

Playing in the Rain

Come out and play.
It's a rainy day
And we'll run between the drops.
Though it's lots of fun
To play in the sun,
Why wait till the shower stops?

If it pours and pours
We can play indoors
But a little rain is nice.
If I bring my soap
Is there any hope
That I won't have to bathe twice?

If it pours and pours
We can play indoors
But a little rain's OK.
We won't melt in the rain
So don't complain.
Say hooray for a rainy day.

Willie the Whale

Here's a short tale
About Willie the Whale,
A sad, sad mammal whose wish
Is to make you agree,
Though he lives in the sea,
A whale isn't really a fish.

He swims, he has fins,
And so he begins
To look like a fish, no doubt.
But a whale's a mammal
Like a cat or camel.
Call Willie a fish and he'll pout.

If I called you a curtain
I'm certainly certain
You'd say "I'm a kid, not a drape."
If I called you a donkey
Or even a monkey,
You'd say "I'm no beast. I'm no ape."

If I called you a rug,
Or a bug, or a slug,
Your feelings I'd surely squish.
So don't hurt poor Willie,
He's no tiger lily,
And he certainly isn't a fish.

Silly Rhymes

Robin, ribbon, ribbity ree
Make some silly rhymes with me.
Snicker, snacker, sniggity snoo.
If I can do it, you can too.

Really, rally, rellipy run.
Don't you think this rhyming's fun?
Wally, wheelie, willowy wow.
I've had my turn. It's your turn now.

 # Spring

The leaves are green, and the sky is blue.
It's a nice warm day, and there's lots to do.

There's not one cloud to hide the sun.
Let's go outdoors and have some fun.

The breeze is brisk, so it's not too hot,
And over there is a shady spot.

The grass is green, and the dirt smells sweet,
So take off your shoes and you'll treat your feet.

The air smells fresh. So what do you say?
Come out and play, it's a pretty day.

Dance Class

Here is how our dance class goes:
Down on your knees, Louise.
Up on your toes, Rose.

We'll be good at this someday.
Do a plié, May.
Do a jeté, Kay.

Crowds of Clouds

Swim through the clouds with me.
Isn't it grand?!
Dive through that puffy one.
Quick! Hold my hand.

Here comes a thundercloud
Boomy and dark.
Watch out for lightning.
See—there's a spark.

Look for a snowcloud.
Watch the snow fall.
Gather it up
And we'll make a snowball.

Float through the skies with me
Without a care.
Close your eyes and pretend
And we're already there.

Submarine Sam

When Submarine Sam goes under the sea,
What kind of view do you think there'll be?
What kind of sights will our sailor see
When Submarine Sam goes under the sea?

Sky Flying

Here am I,
Flying through the sky
Way up high,

Clinging to my kite
On my flight
Through the night.

Traveling very far,
Here we are.
Grab a star.

Soon
We'll pass the moon,
Round as a balloon.

This is fun,
But there's the rising sun.
Our trip is done.

Playing in the Moonlight

Come out and play, come out and play.
The moon is full, and it's bright as day.

Bring your softballs and jump ropes, too.
The moon is lighting the night for you.

We'll play hopscotch beneath the stars.
We'll play marbles and look for Mars.

It's late at night, and there's no one out.
We'll have the street to ourselves, no doubt.

Bring your bike and your bat and ball,
Your trucks and trains—you can bring them all.

The stars are shining to light your way.
The moon is full, so come out and play.

Silly, Soothing
Poems

Elliott Eel

Elliot Eel
Kept trying to kneel
But an eel doesn't have any knees.
Elliot Eel
Let out a loud squeal
And he said, "I want some knees, please!"

But why the big fuss?
An eel, unlike us,
Can bend himself anywhere.
I think it would be
A real treat for me
To slither my way up a stair.

That's a thing, it is true,
That Elliot can do.
And you and I can't do at all.
If I were to try it
It would be a riot
To watch me fail and then fall.

So if Elliot Eel
Is unable to kneel.
It shouldn't matter. No way!
He shouldn't be sad.
And he shouldn't be mad.
I'd trade places with him any day.

Rain Begone

When it rains
John complains.
He hates a rainy day.
He gets upset
If he gets wet
When he goes out to play.

When there's sun
John has fun.
He stays nice and dry.
Are you like John?
Then rain, begone!
Say "Hooray!" for a bright blue sky.

Stevie's Party

Stevie's party was Saturday.
We played some games in a whole new way.
We played Pin the Tail. Steve turned me. I spun.
I felt real dizzy, but it was fun.
I lost my balance and fell down flat
And taped the tail to Stevie's cat!

We bobbed for apples. Steve's grandpa was there.
He tried it himself and lost his hair!
His wig slipped off and fell in the pail.
I'm not making up this outrageous tale!
He fished it out and he tried again
And you won't believe what happened then:
He bit the apple and gave a shout
'Cause his set of false teeth had fallen out!

The kids all laughed, he looked so strange.
Steve's mother said, "We need a change.
We'll try a sack race. Come out in the yard."
We kids were laughing very hard,

But out we went. We got in teams
And jumped in bags. We let out screams.
But Kim screamed loudest, and not in fun.
She left the bag and started to run.
Steve looked in the bag she'd been jumping in.
Wondering what the problem had been.
His pet mouse, Mike, was curled inside.
I wonder if Mike enjoyed the ride?

Steve's mom said, "All of you, come back in.
The clown is here. He's going to begin."
We gave up playing. We didn't want to.
It's the funnest party I've ever gone to.

Extraordinary Jerry

Jerry thinks he's very
Extraordinary.
Just 'cause he can play
In a reasonably good way
Guitar, trombone, kazoo.
Well, I know I can't. Can you?

A Big Dog's Chasing Me

One, two, three,
A big dog's chasing me.
Four, five six,
I hope he only licks.
Seven, eight, nine,
I'm glad he's not a lion.
Ten!
I'm safely home again!

Lull-a-Boy (or Girl): Lullabyes and Other Naptime Ditties

Lullabyes are a traditional way of soothing kids to sleep. Getting beyond "Rock-a-Bye Baby"—the words of which aren't as well suited to a pre-schooler as they are to an infant—there are other songs that are suitable for soothing kids into a restful state. Here are a few written especially for naptime. In addition to being soothing, lulling songs, several of them carry a message for your child: If you take a nap now, your body will have more strength later.

It's Naptime

(Sing this one to the tune of "On Top of Old Smoky")

It's naptime, you're sleepy,
So get into bed,
And soon pretty pictures,
Will fill up your head.

In dreams you own castles,
And live in them too,
And spend your days going
To the beach and the zoo.

When you wake, I'll kiss you,
But now not a peep.
So close your eyes, drift off,
And have a good sleep.

The Naptime Book

Close Your Eyes

(Sing this to the tune of "Twinkle, Twinkle Little Star")

Now it's naptime, close your eyes.
If you sleep you're very wise.
Resting well is awf'ly smart.
It gives you a good head start.
In your sleep you fly on wings.
Close your eyes and dream sweet things.

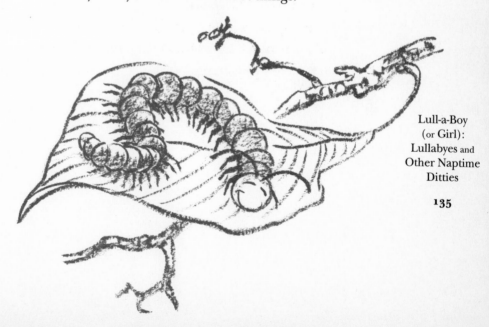

Lull-a-Boy
(or Girl):
Lullabyes and
Other Naptime
Ditties

135

The Energy Song

(Sing this one to the tune of "This Old Man," but sing it more slowly)

If a nice nap you take
You'll feel stronger when you wake.
You'll have lots of energy, strength enough to play,
Zooming onward through the day.

Stay and rest. Take your time.
Think about this little rhyme.
'Cause it makes a point to you, sleeping's what you need.
You'll wake stronger, yes indeed.

Give Your Body a Break

(Sing this one to the tune of "My Old Kentucky Home")

Oh, the day's been fun, but it's time to take a nap,
So you'll have strength later to play.
You're a growing boy/girl, full of energy to spare,
But your body needs a break today.
Oh, sleep awhile, my darling.
Sleep, and wake refreshed.
In your dreams you'll do
Many happy things, I know,
And you'll wake full of new energy and zest.

Lull-a-Boy
(or Girl):
Lullabyes and
Other Naptime
Ditties

Sleep, Sleep Tight

(Sing this one to the tune of "Three Blind Mice,"
but slowly)

Sleep, sleep tight.
Sleep, sleep tight.
Dream happy things.
Dream happy things.
And when you wake up, I'll be right here.
You know your mommy is always near.
'Cause I love you so much, you're very dear,
So sleep, sleep tight.

Close Your Eyes

(Sing this one to the tune of "Row, Row,
Row Your Boat," but slowly)

Close, close, close your eyes.
Drift and dream and rest.
Sleep awhile, sleep awhile, sleep awhile,
  sleep awhile,
That's what I'd suggest.

Sleep, sleep, sleep, my child.
Dream of happy things.
Fly through sleep, fly through sleep, fly through
  sleep, fly through sleep.
Fly on robin's wings.

When, when, when you wake
You'll feel good as new.
Sleep is good, sleep is good, sleep is good,
  sleep is good.
Nap well. I love you.

Lull-a-Boy
(or Girl):
Lullabyes and
Other Naptime
Ditties

139

Travels to the Lands of Imagination and Conceptualization

It's hard for a child to fall asleep when his mind is racing. Give him something pleasant to think about and he'll be much more able to lie there and relax. For some kids, thinking about the circus might be simply intriguing and perfect for drifting into a nap; but for others, it might be too stimulating for pre-naptime, kicking the brain into high gear. And for *any* kid, if an actual visit to the circus is imminent, thoughts of the circus are bound to rev him up.

If you don't have much time to spend with your child when you put him in for a nap, these "travels to the land of imagination and conceptualization" may be your salvation, too. You can tuck him under his special naptime quilt and suggest, "Why don't you think about _____ while you're lying there," then quickly exit and get into the other room where the baby is crying or the goulash sounds like it's boiling over or the doorbell or phone is ringing or the mortgage or rent check needs to be written quickly because the mail carrier will be picking up the mail any time now and the check *has* to go out *today.*

Of course, if you do have time, sit with your child and let him answer you aloud. When he's finished, you can ask him a follow-up question suggested by his initial answer or go on to the next question. Whenever you do leave the room, you can still leave him with one last question to start thinking about in his mind as you kiss him Good Nap.

Here are some questions and suggestions for restful, involved thinking that can occupy your child's mind as he lies there:

- Where do birds fly to have fun? We've never seen bird restaurants and there certainly aren't bird skating rinks! What do birds do for enjoyment?

- What do squirrels do for fun?

❄ Picture a scene that's totally light blue. What do you see? Do you see a blue bird flying in a blue sky, with some blue-tinged clouds? Or do you see something else? See how many more parts you can add to the picture. Concentrate and see it clearly in your mind.

❧ Write a story in your head. You don't have to tell it to me or say it out loud. Just think about it. Work it all out in your head.

❀ Picture yourself meeting your favorite movie or TV character. Imagine talking to that person. What would he or she say to you? What would you say to him or her? Imagine the whole conversation.

⑥ Picture yourself meeting your favorite cartoon or comic book or comic strip character. Imagine talking to that character. What would he or she say to you? What would you say to him or her? Imagine the whole conversation.

✳ If you could talk to anyone in the world and ask him or her any questions you wanted to, who would you talk to and what would you ask that person?

✍ You've heard me sing you a lullabye to the tune of "On Top of Old Smokey." Why don't *you* try to write words to a tune you know? Make up a song in your head.

❦ Dream up a design for a puppet. It could be a sock puppet or a Popsicle-stick puppet or any other kind. How would you make the puppet?

⑥ If you could be Santa and give your friends anything at all that you wanted to for Christmas, what would you give them?

❧ If Santa's reindeer retired, where do you think they would go?

❧ If Santa's reindeer retired, what do you think he would name their replacements?

❀ What do you think some of the names of Santa's elves might be?

❧ Do you really think there's just one tooth fairy, or do you think there's a bunch of them, each one in charge of a certain part of the world? What do you think the tooth fairies' names are? (Or if there's only one, what is her name?)

❋ Is the tooth fairy a girl? Tinkerbell was a girl. The Blue Fairy in Pinocchio was a girl. It seems like *all* the famous fairies are girls. But there must be boy fairies too, don't you think? Do you suppose the boys do other things than the girls do? What do they do?

❧ Where do you think Santa's elves go on vacation when Christmas is over? What do you suppose they do for fun?

❀ Where do you think Santa's elves get *their* Christmas presents from?

◎ Think back as far as you can remember. Try to remember all the things you can from when you were as little as you can remember. And try to remember me holding you and hugging you and comforting you and always loving you.

⚜ If you could travel to anywhere you wanted, where would you go? Why would you choose to go there? What would you do when you got there?

☙ If you could build a playground, what would you put in it that isn't in the playground we usually go to?

❉ If you could have a zoo in the backyard, what animals would you put there, and why?

❉ If you could be any kind of animal, what kind would you be? Why?

◎ Who's your favorite person or animal in a book or story, and why?

✿ What are all the prettiest things you can think of?

 Why do you suppose only men have moustaches and beards but not women?

✤ Why do you suppose dogs and cats can be black or white or brown or gray or blond-colored or orangey (cats anyhow) but never green or purple or bright red or pink?

❀ Try to picture a really funny-looking animal, like a pink horse with feathers where its mane should be. What would another really funny-looking animal look like?

❦ Tell me what the nicest thing is about Grandma. Now, what's the nicest thing about Grandpa? How about [name a neighbor your child likes]? What about your pre-school teacher? How about ____? (On various occasions, you can mention various relatives, friends of the family, local merchants the child knows, babysitters, and others whom the child interacts with. You can even mention people she doesn't especially like, to point out that even people you aren't enthusiastic about have their good points.)

✿ What are some of the nice things you can do for people that will make them feel good inside?

☙ Suppose someone one day went into the jungle and there, hidden away deep among the trees and vines, they discovered a new animal that no one had ever seen before. What do you think it might look like? What do you think they might name it?

❁ If you weren't named ____, what would you call yourself? What middle name would you give yourself?

❧ What's your favorite holiday and why?

❊ If you could celebrate your birthday any way you wanted, how would you celebrate it?

☺ If your favorite person from TV came to our house, what would you show him or her? What do you think he or she would want for dinner? How do you think he or she would want to spend the evening?

❄ If our dog (cat) (the neighbor's dog or cat) could talk, what do you think he would say?

Time Out for Mom Too!

What are *you* going to do while your child is napping? This time to yourself is precious; use it well!

Using the time "well" doesn't need to equate with being industrious, though there's certainly nothing wrong with taking that half-hour or hour of peace and privacy as an opportunity to get something accomplished. On the other hand, there's nothing wrong with indulging yourself in a restful activity either, whether it's taking a nap yourself or some other relaxing interlude.

Either way, you're making good use of the time. Here are a few suggestions for ways to use your child's nap time well for yourself:

🌸 Indulge yourself in the luxury of a looooong shower or bath without having to worry, *What's he getting into while*

I'm in here? Why not make it a bubblebath . . . and bring a tall, cool iced tea into the bathroom with you or a cup of hot cocoa in cold weather.

❀ Take a nap. Not just a rest with "one eye and one ear open," but an honest-to-goodness, restful, relaxing nap. You've had a strenuous day too; aren't you entitled? Yes, you are!

❁ Read part of a good absorbing novel or a funny book. A good pick might be almost anything by the late Erma Bombeck—you can certainly relate to most of what she wrote about!

❦ Stretch out on the sofa with a cool, wet square of paper towel over each of your closed eyes and listen to *your* favorite music instead of your child's favorite CD or tape. Let your mind wander.

❄ Start planning your next vacation—even if it's still months away.

❋ Write that letter—snailmail or email—that you've been promising yourself to write to your friend who lives at a distance from you. When you're writing to her, it will feel almost like a visit with her. Once you've written your letter, you can begin enjoying the anticipation of receiving her letter to you in return.

❧ Leaf through one of your favorite catalogues and order yourself a little indulgence. It doesn't have to be an extravagance, though if what you want is expensive and you can afford to treat yourself to it, great! A small but meaningful knickknack, an outfit you really need and can afford, or an inexpensive paperback book are all indulgences too.

❧ Reflect on all the reasons you really love the mini-tornado you just put in for a nap. She may try your patience; she may be a handful; she may be obstinate or have other less-than-desirable qualities; but now that you have a moment to catch your breath, reflect on all the reasons you love her and focus on *those* now and then again when she wakes up—especially if she's one of those kids who wakes up so cranky that you wonder if a nap is worth it.

❧ Do some relaxing, centering yoga.

❧ Do a relaxation exercise such as closing your eyes, taking deep, calming breaths. Picture yourself in a serene setting such as a peaceful beach where you're lying quietly on the sand absorbing the sun's warming rays while the ocean laps quietly at the shore nearby. Or a deserted meadow where you can lie among the wildflowers smelling sweet and earthy smells while a gentle breeze licks at your bare feet and lightly tickles your face and arms.

❀ Take out your college or high school yearbook, your summer camp memorabilia, photo albums, scrapbooks, or other "treasures" that date back to an earlier time when your life was different (not necessarily *better*, just *different*). Reminisce about times gone by and the fun you had then. You probably wouldn't want to go back to those times, but they had their high points; revisiting them now in memory will give you a much-needed break.

❀ Brew a fresh cup of coffee. Make it special by flavoring it with cinnamon or vanilla or a bit of chocolate, or add a dollop of ice cream. (Be wicked—never mind the calories!) Then settle in to a comfortable chair, do a crossword puzzle, and sip the coffee in peace and luxury.

❀ Start preparations for dinner now while you can work in the kitchen undisturbed and without concern about what your child is up to or about his getting hurt if he's in the kitchen with you. Do as much of the prep work now as you can, minimizing what you'll have to do later when he's awake. (Hint: If you have potatoes to peel and cut but you're concerned about them turning gray-brown, just plop them in water when you've peeled and cut them and they'll hold up nicely.)

⑥ Got a chore waiting for you such as balancing the checkbook, something that requires a great deal of concentration? It's tough to devote your full brain to it when you're keeping an eye on your son or daughter and you're probably usually too tired to do a good job by the time your child is in bed. Why not tackle that task now?!

❋ Similarly, if you have a phone call to make that requires your full attention—a bill you need to dispute, a complaint to your landlord, a speaker you need to engage to address an upcoming meeting of your organization, or something else along those lines, now, while you can talk undisturbed, is a good time to make that call.

✆ If your husband has a job in which he can take personal phone calls without their being an intrusion or a distraction, he'd probably welcome an "I love you" call. A brief conversation with him would probably pick up your spirits too.

✳ Of course, if there's something you want to discuss over the phone with a friend and you need privacy to have the conversation, now's a good time for that.

❦ Do a quick bit of housecleaning while there's no one underfoot. Certainly you can't thoroughly clean the whole house during one naptime, but you *can* pick up the living room, reorganize the fridge, clean the stove top, get a load of wash going, or scrub out the bathroom without your child sticking his hand into the toilet "to help you."

❦ Got a chore you're hesitant to do when your child is running around? Are you afraid to do the ironing for fear he'll charge into the room, pull on the cord (or trip over it), and bring the hot iron down on himself? Is there any other task for which you harbor similar safety concerns? Do you promise yourself daily that you'll do these things when he's in bed, only to find that, by the time you've put him to bed, you're too tired? Do those chores during naptime!

❦ Read a book of poems (or at least part of the book).

❦ Call your mother.

About the Author

Cynthia MacGregor has published more than forty books. Many of them, including *Night-Night* (Conari Press, 2001), offer helpful, not to mention fun, creative, and innovative ideas for parents. "I've been writing most of my life," she says. "And there's no one I'd want to change lives with." A New York native transplanted to Florida, MacGregor writes puns and haiku and cooks up a storm in her spare time. Her web site is *CynthiaMacGregor.com.*

To Our Readers

Conari Press, an imprint of Red Wheel/Weiser, publishes books on topics ranging from spirituality, personal growth, and relationships to women's issues, parenting, and social issues. Our mission is to publish quality books that will make a difference in people's lives—how we feel about ourselves and how we relate to one another. We value integrity, compassion, and receptivity, both in the books we publish and in the way we do business.

Our readers are our most important resource, and we value your input, suggestions, and ideas about what you would like to see published. Please feel free to contact us, to request our latest book catalog, or to be added to our mailing list.

CONARI PRESS
An imprint of Red Wheel/Weiser, LLC
P.O. Box 612
York Beach, ME 03910-0612
www.conari.com